MY CONFESSION
OF FAITH

PERSONAL PRAYERS THAT WILL CHANGE YOUR LIFE

AND

THE WAY YOU SEE THINGS -

MY CONFESSION OF FAITH

C. WAYNE PRATT

NKJV – New King James Version
Scripture taken from the New King James Version. Copyright 1979, 1980, 1982 by Thomas Nelson, inc. Used by permission. All rights reserved.

KJV - King James Version
Scripture taken from the King James Version of the Bible.

This book was printed in the United States of America.

Rev. date: 08/08/2014

To order additional copies of this book, contact:
Xlibris LLC
1-888-795-4274
www.Xlibris.com
Orders@Xlibris.com
663177

Contents

Foreword

Prayers are confessions from our hearts about our lives – how we see ourselves, how we esteem God through Jesus Christ. Many times we pray and we wonder what has become of our prayers. A close examination of our prayers and our attitude before God may reveal that we are neither praying in accordance with God's promises to us nor setting our minds, thoughts and focus on God as we pray. Our minds may be consumed more by our perception of the magnitude of our problems, than by faith in God, the Almighty one, in whom there is all power to solve them.

Out of the mouth of Solomon, the wisest king that ever graced the earth came these words of wisdom from God Himself, "Trust in the Lord with all thine heart; and lean not unto thine own understanding. In all thy ways acknowledge him, and he shall direct thy paths," (Proverbs 3:5-6; KJV). This word is directed to every one of us, as individuals. So that as children of God, we can have a common mindset in our understanding of what He requires of us.

God wants us to go before Him, confident that He is who He says He is; and that He can do all He says He can do. How much better, then, it is to go before Him, praying and bearing His own promises to us, as our terms of reference.

This is exactly what Pastor C. Wayne Pratt, an excellent teacher of the Bible, has done. He has tirelessly searched the Bible for God's promises in every human situation as listed in the inerrant word of God, and he has composed authentic prayers using these promises to us, His human family. These prayers have helped many individuals and families to pray knowing the outcome of prayers based on God's promises. It has helped many to experience peace after a time before God, in dire desperation.

Now they are in your hands, God's promises to us about the things for which we pray. This book is a journey with an experience that will change your life. It will help you to talk to God in a way that confesses your own personal faith.

Kwesi Oginga; B.A.; M.A.
Assoc. Pastor; New Life Ministries
Maryland, USA.

Dear God

Because Your Word says that the tongue has the power of life and death,[1] and that we overcome the devil by the word of our testimony,[2] and since Your Word says "Let the redeemed of the Lord say so,"[3] therefore I, like Ezekiel, will prophesy to the dry bones of my life,[4] and just as Jesus did in the wilderness, I will declare "It is written."[5] The Word of faith is near me—it is in my heart and in my mouth; therefore, with my heart I will believe, and with my mouth I will confess Your Word unto salvation.[6] Because I believe, I also speak—with the same spirit of faith

---

[1] Proverbs 18:21

[2] Revelation 12:11

[3] Psalm 107:2

[4] Ezekiel 37:1-10

[5] Matthew 4:1-11

[6] Romans 10:8-10

I believe and therefore I speak.[7] You spoke the worlds into existence by Your mighty Word, and You call into being things that do not exist.[8] You are ALWAYS watching over Your Word to perform it.[9] Your Word says that my tongue is like the pen of a skillful writer[10] and that I can write Your Word on the tablet of my heart.[11] Regardless of the situations in my life, I declare that You are good ALL the time, and Your mercy and love are everlasting![12] God, it is because of Your great love that we are not consumed; Your compassions NEVER fail—they are new EVERY morning; great is Your faithfulness![13] ALL of Your exceeding great and precious promises[14] are "Yes" in Christ, and we say "Amen" to each and every one of them![15] Your Word is true, forever settled and

[7] 2 Corinthians 4:13

[8] Romans 4:17

[9] Jeremiah 1:12

[10] Psalm 45:1

[11] Proverbs 3:3

[12] Psalm 136:1

[13] Lamentations 3:22-23

[14] 2 Peter 1:4

[15] 2 Corinthians 1:20

firm in heaven[16]—it is IMPOSSIBLE for You to lie![17] Even when we are faithless, You remain faithful.[18]

---

[16] Psalm 119:89

[17] Hebrews 6:18

[18] 2 Timothy 2:13

The Blessing of Abraham

Because I believe in Your Son, Jesus Christ, my Savior and Lord, I am a child of Abraham, and because I have faith, I am blessed along with Abraham.[19] Since I belong to Christ, I am Abraham's seed, and I am an heir according to the promise. Everything that was promised to Abraham is mine through Jesus Christ; like Isaac, I am also a child of promise.[20] As a child of Abraham, You have promised to bless me: my children will be blessed, the works of my hands will be blessed, I will be blessed when I go out and when I come in, my house will be blessed, and my crops will be blessed. You will bless me and make me a blessing to nations.[21] You have blessed me with EVERY spiritual blessing in the heavenly realms in Christ.[22] ALL the peoples on the earth will see

---

[19]   Galatians 3:7-9

[20]   Galatians 3:22; 4:28

[21]   Deuteronomy 28:1-14

[22]   Ephesians 1:3

that I am called by Your Name and they will fear You. You will give me descendants like the stars in the sky, and they will take possession of the cities of their enemies; through them ALL nations on the earth will be blessed. You have made me the head and not the tail. I will ALWAYS be at the top, NEVER at the bottom. I will be fruitful and prosperous, and I will lend to nations but borrow from none. I will have abundant prosperity so that I can be a blessing to many and meet the needs of others. Our barns will be filled with EVERY kind of provision. Our sheep will increase by thousands, by tens of thousands in our fields; there will be NO breaching of walls, NO going into captivity, NO cry of distress in our streets. Blessed are the people whose God is the LORD.[23]

---

[23]   Psalm 144:13-15

Trust in God, not Man

I know it is better to trust in the Lord than to put my confidence in princes.[24] I will fix my eyes on Jesus, the Author and Finisher of my faith.[25] I will not look to man to meet ANY of my needs, but I will trust solely in Him, for My God shall provide ALL my needs according to His glorious riches in Christ Jesus.[26] Like Your servant David, I have NEVER seen the righteous forsaken or their children begging bread.[27] The Lord is my Shepherd, and I shall NEVER be in want.[28] I will depend on the Lord and put my trust and confidence in Him; I will not depend on flesh.[29]

---

[24] Psalm 118:8-9

[25] Hebrews 12:2

[26] Philippians 4:19

[27] Psalm 37:25

[28] Psalm 23:1

[29] Jeremiah 17:5

I will call on the Lord in prayer, knowing that WHATEVER I ask for according to His will, I shall receive.[30] God gives good gifts to those who ask Him[31]—EVERY good and perfect gift comes from the Father of lights, with whom there is no variableness or shadow of turning.[32] There is NOTHING too hard for the Lord[33]—ALL things are possible when I believe. He is able to do immeasurably more than I ask or imagine, according to His power that is at work within me.[34] When I lack wisdom, He will give me His wisdom generously, without finding fault or chiding me.[35] God's Presence is with me ALWAYS, even to the very end of the age.[36] He will NEVER, ever leave me or forsake me; the Lord is my Helper—I will not fear what man can do to me.[37] And God has sent His angels to serve those who will inherit salvation;[38] the angel

---

[30]   Matthew 21:22; John 15:7, 16; 1 John 5:14-15

[31]   Matthew 7:7

[32]   James 1:17

[33]   Genesis 18:14; Jeremiah 32:17

[34]   Ephesians 3:20

[35]   James 1:5

[36]   Matthew 28:20

[37]   Hebrews 13:5-6

[38]   Hebrews 1:14

of the Lord encamps around those who fear Him.[39] The Word of God says let the weak say I am strong.[40] I can do ALL things through Christ who strengthens me.[41] I have been strengthened with power and might by God's Holy Spirit in my inner man.[42]

---

[39]   Psalm 34:7

[40]   Joel 3:10

[41]   Philippians 4:13

[42]   Ephesians 3:15

Victory over Enemies

The Lord will grant that EVERY enemy that rises up against me will be defeated. They will come at me from one direction but flee in seven.[43] Let God arise, and ALL of His enemies be scattered![44] The Lord will march out like a mighty man, like a warrior He will stir up His zeal; with a shout He will raise the battle cry and will triumph over His enemies.[45] God's light shines into the darkness, and the darkness cannot overcome it.[46] Even when the enemy comes in like a flood, the Spirit of the Lord will lift up a standard against him.[47] NO weapon formed against me will prevail and God will refute EVERY tongue that accuses

---

[43] Deuteronomy 28:7

[44] Psalm 68:1

[45] Isaiah 42:13

[46] John 1:5

[47] Isaiah 59:19

me. As a servant of the Lord, this is my heritage, and my vindication comes from the Lord.[48]

Thanks be to God who ALWAYS leads me in His triumph.[49] I believe that Jesus, the Son of God, was manifested to destroy EVERY work of the devil[50] and that through His death on the Cross, He destroyed him who had the power of death, that is, the devil, and freed me from the fear of death.[51] Jesus now holds the keys of hell and death.[52] EVERYONE who is born of God overcomes the world. This is the victory that overcomes the world, even our faith.[53] It is not by human might or power, but by Your Spirit that EVERY mountain and obstacle is flattened.[54] Jesus is building His Church, and the gates of hell CANNOT prevail against it.[55] God has given me authority to trample on snakes and scorpions, and to overcome ALL the power of

---

[48]   Isaiah 54:17

[49]   2 Corinthians 2:14

[50]   1 John 3:8

[51]   Hebrews 2:14-15

[52]   Revelation 1:17-18

[53]   1 John 5:4

[54]   Zechariah 4:6-7

[55]   Matthew 16:18

the enemy; NOTHING will harm me.[56] I am strong in the Lord and in His mighty power—I put on the whole armor of God, and take my stand against the devil's schemes.[57] I know that when I resist the devil, he MUST flee from me.[58]

---

[56]   Luke 10:19

[57]   Ephesians 6:10-18

[58]   James 4:7

No Condemnation

I am a new creation in Christ—ALL of the old things have passed away, and ALL things have become new in my life.[59] ALL of my past sins have been forgiven and cast into the sea of God's forgetfulness.[60] My sins and iniquities He will remember no more.[61] I am the righteousness of God in Christ,[62] justified by the blood of Jesus,[63] so I can now come boldly into the Most Holy Place in full assurance of faith by His blood.[64] There is NO condemnation for those who are in Christ. As one of God's chosen, NO ONE can bring ANY charge against me. Because God is for me, who can be against me? I believe Christ Jesus died for

---

[59] 2 Corinthians 5:17

[60] Micah 7:19

[61] Hebrews 10:17

[62] 2 Corinthians 5:21

[63] Romans 5:9

[64] Hebrews 10:19-22

me, was raised to life, and right now is sitting at the right hand of God interceding for me. NOTHING can separate me from the love of Christ. In ALL situations, at ALL times, I am more than a conqueror through Him who loved me.[65]

---

[65]   Romans 8:1, 31-39

Freedom, Health and Healing

Because Jesus has set me free, I am free indeed[66]—free from sin, oppression, sickness and infirmity, religious yokes and bondages, and anything else that would try to hinder my walk and service for God. The anointing of God's Spirit has broken EVERY yoke in my life.[67] Where the Spirit of the Lord is, there is liberty![68] God has delivered me out of the hands of ALL my enemies so that I might serve Him without fear, in holiness and righteousness ALL the days of my life.[69]

I have been redeemed out of the hands of the enemy through the blood of Jesus— therefore, my body, soul, mind, and spirit belong to God. The devil has NO power or claim to my life. My body is the

---

[66] John 8:36

[67] Isaiah 10:27

[68] 2 Corinthians 3:17

[69] Luke 1:74-75

temple of the Holy Spirit.[70] God has promised health and prosperity for my body, even as my soul prospers.[71] By the stripes on Jesus' back, I was healed.[72] God's name is "Jehovah Rapha," the Lord who heals me of ALL sickness and disease.[73] I will bless the Lord at ALL times, and forget not ALL of His benefits—He forgives ALL of my sins, heals ALL of my diseases, redeems my life from the pit, crowns me with love and compassion, satisfies my desires with good things, and renews my youth like the eagle's.[74] I will enjoy long life, living out the full number of my days ordained in God's Book.[75] The same Spirit that raised Christ from the dead is dwelling in me, and He will quicken my mortal body.[76]

---

[70] 1 Corinthians 3:16

[71] 3 John 2

[72] Isaiah 53:5

[73] Exodus 15:26

[74] Psalm 103:1-5

[75] Psalm 91:16; 139:16

[76] Romans 8:11

Sound Mind

God has not given me a spirit of fear, but of power, love, and a sound and disciplined mind.[77] I take captive every wandering, evil thought, any argument or pretension that sets itself against the knowledge of God, and make it obedient to Christ. I cast down every imagination and every high thing in my mind that exalts itself against the knowledge of God, for the weapons of my warfare are not carnal but mighty through God to pulling down and demolishing strongholds.[78] I will not be anxious in my mind, for the peace of God which transcends all understanding will guard my heart and mind in Christ Jesus. Whatever is true, noble, right, pure, lovely, admirable, excellent or praiseworthy—I will think about such things.[79]

---

[77]   2 Timothy 1:7

[78]   2 Corinthians 10:4-5

[79]   Philippians 4:6-8

Sleep and Rest

Lord, You have promised a Sabbath rest for Your people.[80] You called the weary and the burdened to come to You, and You said You would give them rest.[81] You send abundant showers of rain to refresh Your people when they are weary.[82] I cease from striving, vain ambition, and self motivated work, and I enter Your rest. You have promised sleep for Your beloved.[83] Even in the midst of trouble, I lie down in peace, and sleep. For You sustain me, and make me dwell in safety.[84] When I lie down, I will not be afraid—I will have NO fear of disaster or ruin. My sleep will be sweet, for You, Lord, will be my confidence, and You will

---

[80]   Hebrews 4:1-11eH

[81]   Matthew 11:28

[82]   Psalm 68:9

[83]   Psalm 127:2

[84]   Psalm 3:5; 4:8

keep my foot from being snared.[85] I cast ALL my cares upon You, for You care for me.[86]

---

[85] Proverbs 3:24-26

[86] 1 Peter 5:7

God's Favor

Lord, You have promised to bless the righteous and surround them with favor as with a shield.[87] You bestow favor and honor, and withhold NO good thing from those whose walk is blameless.[88] NOW is the time of God's favor[89]—Your favor is resting upon me today[90] and it will last for a lifetime.[91] You have lavished me with the riches of Your grace, along with ALL wisdom and understanding.[92] Like Your Son Jesus when He was here on earth, I will have favor with God and with

---

[87] Psalm 5:12

[88] Psalm 84:11

[89] 2 Corinthians 6:2

[90] Psalm 90:17

[91] Psalm 30:5

[92] Ephesians 1:8

men.[93] As one of Your chosen, I will enjoy favor with ALL people.[94] You will bring faithful and godly friends into my life with whom I will enjoy genuine fellowship,[95] friends who will be loyal even in times of adversity[96] who will stick closer than a brother.[97] I will experience harmony and unity with all of my Christian brethren.[98] I claim peace in all of my relationships. You will make even my enemies to be at peace with me as I seek to please You.[99] As far as it concerns me, I will live at peace with ALL men.[100]

---

[93] Luke 2:52

[94] Acts 2:47

[95] 1 John 1:7

[96] Proverbs 17:17

[97] Proverbs 18:24

[98] Psalm 133:1

[99] Proverbs 16:7

[100] Romans 12:18

Hope in Discouragements

The Lord has said that ANYONE who hopes or trusts in Him will NEVER be put to shame or disappointed.[101] Hope does not disappoint us, because God has poured His love into our hearts by the Holy Spirit.[102] Even when I am sad or downcast, God will lift my head[103]— His everlasting arms are underneath me.[104] And even if I fall, the Lord will lift me up and I will stand, for the Lord is able to make me stand.[105] He is able to keep me from falling, and to present me before His glorious presence without fault and with great joy.[106] I will not be downcast or troubled, for I have hope in God. Even though the fig tree

---

[101]   Isaiah 49:23; Romans 10:11

[102]   Romans 5:5

[103]   Psalm 3:3

[104]   Deuteronomy 33:27

[105]   Romans 14:4

[106]   Jude 24

doesn't blossom, and there be no fruit on the vine, and all of the crops fail, yet I will rejoice in the Lord. I will be joyful in God my Savior for He is my strength, and He makes my feet like the feet of a deer, enabling me to go on the heights.[107]

Like Abraham, I will hope against all hope, facing hopeless and impossible situations in my life. I will not weaken in faith or waver in unbelief, for I am fully persuaded that WHATEVER God has promised, HE IS ABLE to perform![108] The God of hope is filling me with ALL joy and peace as I trust in Him, and I am overflowing with hope by the power of the Holy Spirit.[109] Though I do not see Him right now, I love Him and believe in Him, and I am filled with inexpressible and glorious joy, as I look forward to my eternal inheritance, kept in heaven for me, that can never perish, spoil or fade. I have a living hope![110]

---

[107] Habakkuk 3:17-19

[108] Romans 4:18-21

[109] Romans 15:13

[110] 1 Peter 1:3-9

Fruit of the Spirit

Because I am filled with the Spirit, living and led by the Spirit, I will not gratify the desires of the sinful nature. The flesh, with all of its lusts and selfish desires, has been crucified with Christ.[111] I am dead and buried with Him, risen now to walk in newness of life.[112] Because of His New Covenant promises, God has removed my old, stony heart, and has given me a new heart and a new spirit. He has put His Spirit within me, and is now moving and causing me to follow His laws and statutes.[113] He has put His law into my mind, and written it on my heart, so that I can know Him.[114] I have the fruit of the Spirit, which is love, joy, peace, patience, kindness, goodness, faithfulness, gentleness and self-control.[115]

---

[111] Galatians 2:20

[112] Romans 6:1-7

[113] Ezekiel 36:26-27

[114] Jeremiah 31:33-34

[115] Galatians 5:16-23

God has shed His love abroad in my heart by His Holy Spirit,[116] and He is making that love increase and overflow for all people.[117]

I put off all anger, rage, bitterness, unwholesome talk, slander, gossip and lying, and I put on the new self which is being renewed in the knowledge of the image of my Creator. I am being made new in the attitude of my mind and I put on the new self, created to be like God in true righteousness and holiness.[118] I clothe myself with compassion, kindness, humility, gentleness, patience, and forgiveness.[119] My conversation will ALWAYS be full of grace,[120] edifying, building up, and benefiting others according to their needs.[121] EVERY DAY, I am being transformed into His likeness with ever-increasing glory by God's power.[122] My whole spirit, soul and body are being sanctified through and through.[123] He who began the good work in me will complete it

---

[116] Romans 5:5

[117] 1 Thessalonians 3:12

[118] Ephesians 4:23-24

[119] Colossians 3:13

[120] Colossians 4:6

[121] Ephesians 4:29

[122] 2 Corinthians 3:18

[123] 1 Thessalonians 5:23-24

for the day of Christ.[124] The Lord will fulfill His purpose for me, and will NEVER abandon the works of His hands.[125]

---

[124] Philippians 1:6

[125] Psalm 138:8

God's Purpose

I know that ALL things are working together for good in my life because I love God, and I have been called according to His purpose.[126] I know that God has plans for me, plans to prosper me and not to harm me, to give me a hope and a future.[127] The Sovereign Lord God Almighty forever rules over the universe, and His plans and purposes stand firm forever.[128] He does whatever He pleases with the powers of heaven and the peoples of the earth, and NO ONE can hold back His hand.[129] I have been redeemed from the empty, vain way of life handed down to me from my forefathers.[130] My life is now filled with purpose, and my

---

[126] Romans 8:28

[127] Jeremiah 29:11

[128] Psalm 33:11

[129] Daniel 4:35-36

[130] 1 Peter 1:18

labor in the Lord is not in vain.[131] Whatever I sow I shall reap—there will be a rich harvest for the seed I have sown.[132] I know that when I sow generously, I will also reap generously. God is making ALL grace abound to me so that in ALL things, at ALL times, having ALL I need, I will abound in EVERY good work. He is supplying seed for sowing and bread for food, and increasing my store of seed and enlarging my harvest. I am being made rich in EVERY way so that I can be generous on EVERY occasion.[133]

---

[131] 1 Corinthians 15:58

[132] Galatians 6:7-9

[133] 2 Corinthians 9:6-11

Gifts and Ministry

I have the anointing of the Holy Spirit upon my life, and that anointing remains in me.[134] The manifestation of the Spirit, and the gifts of the Spirit, have been given to me for the edification of God's people.[135] I do not lack ANY spiritual gift, as I wait for the coming of the Lord.[136] God will testify to my life and ministry with signs, wonders, miracles, gifts of the Holy Spirit,[137] and a demonstration of the Spirit's power, so that people's faith will not rest on men's wisdom but on God's power.[138] In Jesus' name I will cast out demons, speak in new tongues, pick up

---

[134] 1 John 2:27

[135] 1 Corinthians 12:7

[136] 1 Corinthians 1:7

[137] Hebrews 2:4

[138] 1 Corinthians 2:4-5

snakes, and if I drink ANY deadly poison, it will not hurt me AT ALL. I will lay hands on the sick, and they will get well.[139]

I am not competent in myself for any ministry, but He has made me competent as a minister of the New Covenant by His Spirit.[140] He has equipped me with EVERY good thing for doing His will, and is working in me that which is pleasing in His sight.[141] I know that the power is not in the messenger but in the Message—I am not ashamed of the Gospel, for it is the power of God unto salvation for EVERYONE who believes.[142] God is opening doors of opportunity for me that NO ONE can close, and God will close ALL doors that He does not want opened for me.[143] I will be an instrument for noble purposes, useful to the Master, prepared for EVERY good work.[144] When I go out to minister, I am sure that, wherever I go, I shall go in the fullness of the blessing of

[139] Mark 16:16-20

[140] 2 Corinthians 3:5-6

[141] Hebrews 13:20-21

[142] Romans 1:16-17

[143] Revelation 3:7-8

[144] 2 Timothy 2:21

the Gospel of Christ.[145] I am the salt of the earth, and the light of the world.[146] My life will impact the world and people around me.

---

[145] Romans 15:29

[146] Matthew 5:14-16

Children & Family

Lord, You have promised to bless our children.[147] Children are a heritage from the Lord and they are our reward. They are like arrows in the hands of a warrior, launched against the enemy. They will not be put to shame.[148] You have promised that the children of Your servants will live in Your presence, and even their descendants will be established before You.[149] The children of those who fear the Lord will be mighty in the land and their generation will be blessed.[150] Our sons in their youth will be like well-nurtured plants, and our daughters will be like pillars carved to adorn a palace.[151] You have promised that ALL of our children will

---

[147] Psalm 37:26; Proverbs 20:7

[148] Psalm 127:3-5

[149] Psalm 102:28

[150] Psalm 112:1-2

[151] Psalm 144:12

be taught by the Lord,[152] and that when we train up a child in the way he should go, when he is old, he will NOT depart from it.[153] Lord, just as David prayed for his son Solomon, so we pray that You would give our children wholehearted devotion to keep Your commands.[154] We will not bear children doomed to trouble and misfortune, for they will be a people blessed by the Lord.[155]

Just as the blood of the Passover lamb saved the entire Israelite family, protecting everyone in the household[156], so You have promised that when we believe on the Lord Jesus Christ, our Passover Lamb,[157] we will be saved, and our ENTIRE household.[158] You want ALL of our children, as well as ALL of our extended family, to be saved, for You want ALL men to be saved and to come to the knowledge of the truth.[159] You do not want ANYONE to perish but for EVERYONE to

---

[152] Isaiah 54:13

[153] Proverbs 22:6

[154] 1 Chronicles 29:19

[155] Isaiah 65:23

[156] Exodus 12

[157] 1 Corinthians 5:7

[158] Acts 16:31

[159] 1 Timothy 2:4

come to repentance.[160] The promise of Your Holy Spirit is for us and our children.[161] You promised to pour out Your Spirit on our offspring and Your blessing on our descendants, and they will say "I belong to the Lord."[162] Our sons and daughters will prophesy.[163] According to Your covenant, "Your Spirit is upon us and the words You have put in our mouth will not depart from our mouth or from the mouths of our children or from the mouths of their descendants."[164]

ALL our children will obey and honor their parents, so that it will go well with them, and they will enjoy long life on the earth. They will be brought up in the training and the instruction of the Lord.[165] As believing parents, we know that our children are not unclean—they are sanctified and holy.[166] As elders in the church, we declare that our children will believe, and will not be open to the charge of being wild

---

[160]   2 Peter 3:9

[161]   Acts 2:39

[162]   Isaiah 44:3-5

[163]   Acts 2:17

[164]   Isaiah 59:21

[165]   Ephesians 6:1-3

[166]   1 Corinthians 7:14

and disobedient.[167] They will make wise choices, walking in the fear of God, fleeing youthful lusts, immorality, obscenity, filthy and foolish talk, gossip and slander, drunkenness, greed and idolatry.[168] They will pursue righteousness, faith, love and peace, along with those who call on the Lord out of a pure heart.[169] They will be examples for the believers in speech, in life, in love, in faith and in purity.[170]

When our children are tempted to leave Your path, Your Holy Spirit will convict them of sin, righteousness and judgment.[171] You will block their path with thorns, and wall them in so that they cannot find their way. If they chase after forbidden things, they will not catch them; then they will realize that Your path was better, and return to You in true repentance.[172] You will grant them repentance leading to the knowledge of the truth, and You will bring them to their senses, so they can escape the trap of the devil.[173] Your Word will be a lamp to their feet and a light

---

[167] Titus 1:6

[168] Ephesians 5:3-5

[169] 2 Timothy 2:22

[170] 1 Timothy 4:12

[171] John 16:7

[172] Hosea 2:6-7

[173] 2 Timothy 2:25-26

for their path, continually calling them back to the right way.[174] Your Word is living and powerful, sharper than any two-edged sword, and will bring conviction and the fear of the Lord deep within their heart.

Lord, You will surround our children with good company, for bad company corrupts good morals.[175] They will exercise caution and godly discernment when choosing friends.[176] They will walk with the wise and grow wise, and NOT be a companion of fools.[177] Our children will NOT walk in the counsel of the wicked, but will find their delight in the Law of the Lord.[178] If sinners try to entice them into wrongdoing, they will not give in to negative peer pressure.[179] And because You do not want our children to be unequally yoked in marriage, You will bring the right believer at the appropriate time into our child's life for marriage.[180] You desire that our children and their spouses be one in flesh and spirit,

[174] Psalm 119:105

[175] 1 Corinthians 15:33

[176] Proverbs 12:26

[177] Proverbs 13:20

[178] Psalm 1:1-2

[179] Proverbs 1:10

[180] 2 Corinthians 6:14

because You are seeking godly offspring.[181] Just as Abraham sought a

godly wife for his son Isaac,[182] so we desire that our children, sons and

daughters of Abraham, should marry born-again believers. Our children

will be safe and secure, protected from harm and danger—NO evil or

accidents can befall them outside of God's perfect will.[183]

---

[181]   Malachi 2:15

[182]   Genesis 24:3-4

[183]   Psalm 91

Thanksgiving and Praise

I will bless the Lord AT ALL TIMES; His praise will ALWAYS be on my lips.[184] It is good to give thanks to the Lord—in EVERY circumstance and situation, I will give thanks, for this is God's will for me in Christ Jesus. I will be joyful ALWAYS, continually offering up the sacrifice of praise to my God! Let EVERYTHING that has breath praise the Lord!

---

[184] Psalm 34:1

He is the Rock, His works are perfect,

And all His ways are just.

A faithful God who does no wrong,

Upright and just is He.[185]

Because of the LORD'S great love we are not consumed,

For His compassions never fail.

They are new every morning;

Great is Your faithfulness.[186]

Worthy is the Lamb, who was slain,

To receive power and wealth and wisdom and strength

And honor and glory and praise!

To Him who sits on the throne and to the Lamb

Be praise and honor and glory and power,

For ever and ever![187]

---

[185]   Deuteronomy 32:4

[186]   Lamentations 3:22-23

[187]   Revelation 5:12-13

CPSIA information can be obtained at www.ICGtesting.com
Printed in the USA
BVOW02s0103050815

411777BV00002B/204/P

9 781499 060287